Published by:
Teri Woods Publishing, LLC
P.O. Box 478
New York, NY 10026
www.teriwoodskids.com

Written By: Teri Woods
Illustrated By: Blueberry Illustrations
Character Development By: Katherine McCutcheon

Copyright: TXu-1-904-033
ISBN: 978-0-9857641-2-8
Printed in India

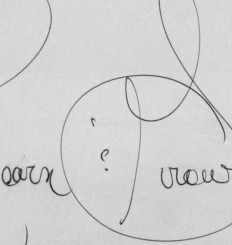

Teri Woods Publishing, LLC © 2014

Dedicated to

_____

My three children, who inspire me and make me so proud. Always be the best you can be,

-Mommy

"AHHH CHOO! God Bless me, please!"

"Oh Lucas, that's a really big sneeze. You need a tissue, I do believe," says Ginger Giraffe.

"Thank you, thank you, for helping my sneeze."

"Well, that's what friends do when someone's in need," says Ginger.

"To be a good friend, you have to help people out. And when you don't agree, don't argue and don't SHOUT," says Big Bear.

"Yes, being kind to others is the smart thing to do, if you want others to be kind to you," says Professor Toad Smart.

"Well, what if others aren't kind to you?" says Lucas.

"Then I'd let them be, I'd find a better friend for me," says Ginger Giraffe.

"That's absolutely the smart thing to do. Find a friend that will be nice to you," says Toad Smart.

"Making smart choices is the way to go. Making the wrong choice is a big no no."

"Values and morals help you do what's right and by making smart choices you'll have a good life."

"What's values and morals and what store are they in?"

"Katie, values cannot be bought. You can only find them inside your heart," says Ginger Giraffe.

"And morals will help guide your life, so you can make smart choices to choose what's right," says Toad Smart.

"Well, I want values and morals inside my heart. I want to make the right choices and I want to be smart."

"I wish I knew what I should do to have values and morals, but I don't have a clue," says Katie Kangaroo.

"PLEASE SOMEONE TELL HER SHE HASN'T GOT A CLUE!" yell the animals.

"Don't you worry, it will be okay, just say these words, and everybody repeat after me," says Ginger.

"Sharing is caring and I want to be nice, I want to have a really good life."

"I want values and morals to be the best I can be and I know money is nice, but it's not everything."

"I promise to be the best I can be, never hurt others and never be a bully."

I promise to read, learn, grow and share
with others all that I know.

I promise to be the best I can be, not only for myself but for EVERYBODY!

About the Author

Teri Woods is a New York Times Best Selling Author and owner of Teri Woods Publishing, which publishes urban fiction and children's books. She loves to write books for people to read and she deeply enjoys putting the books together as a publisher. She has sold millions of books around the world.

The Lucas and Brandon's Magical Playroom book series highlights her two sons. As well as, the characters she has created from the stuffed animals inside their room.

Currently, she is in the process of writing her fifth children's book and she is working on publishing her second book from the Lucas and Brandon's Magical Playroom series.

About Blueberry Illustrations

Blueberry Illustrations is one of the finest illustration companies in the world. Mainly into children book illustrations, Blueberry illustrations' works have won many international awards and many great children's books are being illustrated every year. So far, 112 books have been illustrated and published and many are under making. Every book that is done here is a very special book, as our books bring smiles to the faces of millions of children. To know more and to contact us, please visit **www.blueberryillustrations.com.**

Animal Character Designer: Katherine McCutcheon

Katherine McCutcheon is an illustrator and graphic designer studying at Cazenovia College in New York where she will graduate with a BFA in Visual Communications in May 2015. She began drawing as a child in her home town of Annandale, NJ and aspires to utilize her talent as she pursues a career in the creative fields of graphic design and freelance illustration. To see Katherine's portfolio, please visit **www.kmccgraphics.com.**